2002

Frontispiece

ALPHONSE MARIE MUCHA (1860-1939)

La Blonde and *La Brunette*. 1901, monochrome hand-coloured
lithograph 18" x 13"
(from Alphonse Mucha, Posters and Photographs, Academy Editions,
1971.)

Documents Décoratifs was published in response to an immense
demand for Mucha's designs in the applied arts. The seventy-two
plates are a source book for students of his style. This illustration is
reproduced from Mucha's own hand-coloured version.

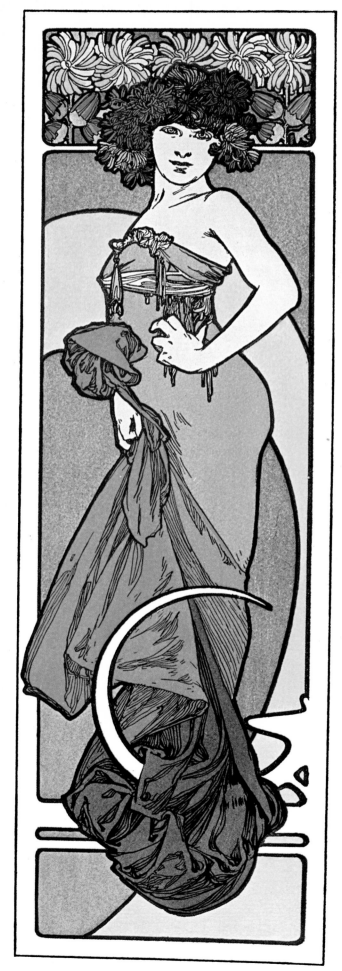

ART NOUVEAU
POSTERS AND DESIGNS

edited by

Andrew Melvin

ACADEMY EDITIONS

We should like to thank the Victoria and Albert Museum for permission to reproduce illustrations; Marlborough Graphics for providing material from their exhibition of Secessionist painters and Mr. Godfrey Pilkington of the Piccadilly Gallery for his advice and help in supplying photographs for reproduction.

First published by Academy Editions, 7a Holland Street, London, W8

© 1971 Academy Editions

Printed by Lowe & Brydone (Printers) Ltd.

INTRODUCTION

Art Nouveau is a term that can be used to classify any one of a dozen styles in Western applied and fine art — each one apparently unique and self-contained, yet all part of a movement that was linked to a determination to shock, to revolt, and above all, to change. The growing homogeneity of Western civilization is evidenced by the speed at which Art Nouveau grew, for the movement hardly lasted thirty years — from about 1885 until the first world war — and it was past its peak of inventiveness half way through that time.

Throughout Europe a host of different names bore witness to the new style. Thus in France it was known as Style Moderne, or Style Nouille (because of the noodle-like tresses of hair that adorned the girls in most Art Nouveau posters). In Germany, it was known as Jugendstil, in Austria as Sezessionstil and in Spain as Modernista. The term Art Nouveau itself was invented only in 1895 when Samuel Bing opened up his shop "La Maison de l'Art Nouveau" in Paris.

Art Nouveau — if these things can be said to start in any one place — started in England. England was the natural breeding ground for such an artistic revolt, for in the second half of the nineteenth century William Morris and his Arts and Crafts movement, the Pre-Raphaelites, and the Aesthetic movement, for all their failings reacted not only against tawdry neo-classicism and academic traditionalism but tried to bring art to terms with the machine age. It is through these revolutionary art movements that the long sinuous line — like a whiplash — that is the hallmark of Art Nouveau was inherited from William Blake.

The emergence and continued existence of the new style, which, with all its trappings of sly and dandified decadence was as much opposed to the Arts and Crafts movement and the Pre-Raphaelites as these movements were to those that had preceeded them is above all the product of two men: Arthur Heygate Mackmurdo, and Aubrey Vincent Beardsley. Both Mackmurdo and Beardsley started their otherwise totally different artistic careers as followers of Morris and the Pre-Raphaelites.

Mackmurdo later on set up an architectural practice and started the *Hobby-Horse* (plate 43). This magazine was the journal of the Century Guild — the first group to revolt from Morris whose once-revolutionary return to gothic was stultifying into conservative historicism. One of Mackmurdo's earliest designs was for a book cover for 'Wren's City Churches' (plate 42). In ten years time this would be the model for a completely new style. Plates 38 and 39 show how introverted and narcissistic that style was to become — without ever quite loosing the essential qualities of Mackmurdo's design.

Beardsley's life seems rather like a reflection of the life of the whole Art Nouveau movement. He lived for only twenty-eight years and drew only during the last six or seven of those, after being encouraged by Burne-Jones. Beardsley succeeded in establishing a completely new style in which the decorative value of line dividing plane surfaces replaced the three-dimensional representation of reality; an emphasis which was fundamental to the development of Art Nouveau and from Beardsley is adopted by artists as diverse as Bradley and Klimt.

The influence on Art Nouveau which makes it more than just part of the ever-changing and evolving art scene is the effect of the introduction of Japanese art to Europe. In the middle eighteen-fifties trade with Japan began, and in exchange for European investment in the far east, Japanese prints, woodcuts and objects of all sorts flowed into Paris and London. The value of Japanese art was that in presenting an entirely different graphic tradition, it gave artists a new starting point for the development of a style no longer based solely on their European artistic inheritance. The flat, nervous faces in Toulouse-Lautrec's posters, the perspectiveless mosaics of Beardsley and the linear development of drapery on Mucha's women are all witnesses to this new catalyst.

The extraordinary vitality of Art Nouveau, while it lasted, can be seen by the immediate way in which it grew from its British and Japanese origins and became the national style of so many different countries.

The Art Nouveau of France was distinguished, in that it was only in that country that it took on a primarily applied form. Underground stations, furniture, and above all bibelots, jewellery and glass became infused with the new writhing and twisting plastic plant forms; the work of Gallé and Guimard became famous throughout the world, and also the newly built avenues and boulevards of Paris had their emptiness filled up by a wealth of multi-coloured posters.

In Vienna, the only apparent connection between Sezessionstil and Western Art Nouveau was the sense of violent revolt that accompanied the two. This was even stronger in Vienna than in England because the Austrian revolt lacked the cushioning effect of the Pre-Raphaelites and the Arts and Crafts movement. The Vienna Secession building which was built in 1898 has engraved above the main doorway the words "To each time its own art: to that art its freedom". This was the slogan of revolution in a city where almost every single public building aped the renaissance in the most superficial way possible.

In the German Empire too, the reaction against the lack of artistic sensibility not only of the Prussian aristocracy but of the new middle class had started. Jugendstil began in Munich with the tapestries of Herman Obrist and soon took on a form not unlike floral English Art Nouveau. Its leading artist was Otto Eckmann (plates 34 and 36) after whose death a new and abstract, almost architectural, style grew up.

The impact of Austro-German Art Nouveau was caused in part by its seriousness; for where the French produced hundreds of gay, and colourful posters and thousands of objects d'art and bibelots, the Secessionists especially were determined to carefully build up a whole revolutionary way of life in which literally every object with which man is in contact in his daily life — whether a lavatory seat of an underground station, was designed to meet the ideals of the Secession. In no other parts of the world did the apostles of the new art achieve anything like the savagery, and violence of Schiele or the high principles of the Secession.

To say that Art Nouveau was killed off by the first world war, as so many of its artists were, is basically true, in that the style certainly did not survive it—but the war and Art Nouveau were products of very much the same social forces. Since the defeat of Napoleon, growing industrialization was changing the basis of European society; the spread of nationalism, socialism and communism challenged the accepted structures of political power. Yet apart from occasional tremors and upheavals such as the events of 1848, the outward forms of law, bureaucracy and government in Europe remained basically unchanged — ossified in the conservative reaction that followed Waterloo. Just as the first world war was the final deadly political symptom of this dichotomy — a bloodletting that finally rid Europe of the old empires, so was Art Nouveau an earlier intellectual symptom.

But where Art Nouveau was unique amongst all the art movements was in its combination of old and new. Art Nouveau represented a combination of the innocent strength of the new forces together with the experienced but dying taste of the old. It was the only non-violent release of tension that could be allowed in European society. This was to some extent recognised. Mucha's posters were considered by many to be part of a plot to corrupt the young. The Austrian Emperor, Franz Joseph was so outraged by Secessionist architecture that he forbade his coachmen ever to drive past Adolf Loos' buildings. The public indignation at the time of the Wilde trials was such that the *Yellow Book* offices were stoned and one reviewer referring to Beardsley's drawings, publicly expressed the view that 'this sort of thing' should be suppressed by act of Parliament. So although Art Nouveau had an irreproachable artistic pedigree, it must be seen for what it was — the last sign of life in a dying society.

LIST OF PLATES

1	Privat-Livemont	Bitter Oriental
2	Privat-Livemont	Cabourg
3	Privat-Livemont	Absinthe Robette
4	Alexandre Steinlen	Yvette Guilbert
5	Alexandre Steinlen	Le Chat Noir
6	Alphonse Mucha	Paris 1900
7	Realier-Dumas	Paris-Mode
8	Toulouse-Lautrec	Reine de Joie
9	Toulouse Lautrec	Troupe de Mademoiselle Eglantine
10	Eugène Grasset	Encre Marquet
11	Eugène Grasset	Grafton Gallery
12	Eugène Grasset	Heroin Addict
13	Will Bradley	Victor Bicycles, Overman Wheel Co.
14	Will Bradley	Victor Bicycles
15	Will Bradley	The Chap-Book
16	Alastair	Lulu
17	Alastair	Carmen
18	Raymond Perry	The Inland Printer
19	Rouville	Moulin Rouge
20	Anon.	Book Cover
21	William Horton	The Way of a Soul (i)
22	William Horton	The Way of a Soul (ii)
23	Aubrey Beardsley	The Houses of Sin
24	Aubrey Beardsley	The Three Musicians
25	Aubrey Beardsley	The Yellow Book
26	Wilhelm List	Strahlenküsse
27	Hans Wacik	The Midnight Feast
28	Carl Moll	Hohe Wart
29	Leopold Stolba	Girl under a Tree
30	Friedrich Konig	Jupiter
31	Fernand Andri	December
32	Rudolf Jettmar	Roman Ruins in Schönbrunn
33	Angelo Jank	Jugend
34	Otto Eckmann	Jugend
35	Leopold Stolba	February
36	Otto Eckmann	The Crab
37	Owen Jones	Wallpaper
38	Anon.	Cotton Cloth
39	Anon.	Cotton Cloth
40	Charles Annesley Voysey	Decorative Fabric
41	Arthur Heygate Mackmurdo	Cotton Cloth
42	Arthur Heygate Mackmurdo	Wren's City Churches
43	Arthur Heygate Mackmurdo	The Hobby Horse
44	Charles Ricketts	Nimphidia and the Muses Elizium
45	The Studio	Pictorial Alphabets
46	The Studio	Pictorial Alphabets
47	Jessie M. King	The Dryad of the Trees
48	Jessie M. King	Her Face was Veiled with a Veil of Gauze . . . .
49	Charles Roberts	Thinking of Little Alice
50	Walter Crane	The Daffodil
51	Walter Crane	The Lillies
52	Charles Ricketts	The Moon-Horned Io

1   PRIVAT-LIVEMONT (b 1861)

Bitter Oriental. 1895, Lithograph, 43½" x 32½"
(Victoria & Albert Museum)

Born in Belgium, Privat-Livemont entered art school when he was thirteen and by 1840 had started his own studio in Brussels. His output was especially prolific in the nineties, his posters of this period reflecting the distinctive style established by Mucha shortly before.

In *Bitter Oriental,* the decorative treatment of hair, the cabalistic symbolism and the horseshoe arch derive directly from Mucha. Less elegantly drawn and intricately composed than Mucha's posters, those of Privat-Livemont had, perhaps, a more immediate impact on the hoardings.

2   **PRIVAT-LIVEMONT (b 1861)**

Cabourg.1896, photo-chromo-lithograph from *Les Maîtres de l'Affiche,* Chaix, 1900 (Victoria & Albert Museum)

The influence of Japanese art of Art Nouveau is here exemplified in the two-dimensional treatment of the waves, probably based on Hokusai's print, *The Wave.* Cabourg was once a rival to Deauville as a Parisian holiday resort.

3   PRIVAT-LIVEMONT (b 1861)

Absinthe Robette. 1896, lithograph (Victoria & Albert Museum)

This poster, published shortly before absinthe was declared an illegal drink throughout Europe, is typical of Privat-Livemont's adaptation of Mucha's style.

4   THEOPHILE-ALEXANDRE STEINLEN (1859-1923)

Yvette Guilbert. Lithograph, 72" x31" (Victoria & Albert Museum)

Steinlen lived in Montmartre for most of his life and was a close
friend of the singer Yvette Guilbert. A convinced socialist, the
subject matter of his paintings was largely drawn from the streets and
characters of Montmartre but his commercial posters usually
featured cats, which he loved, or his daughter, Colette.

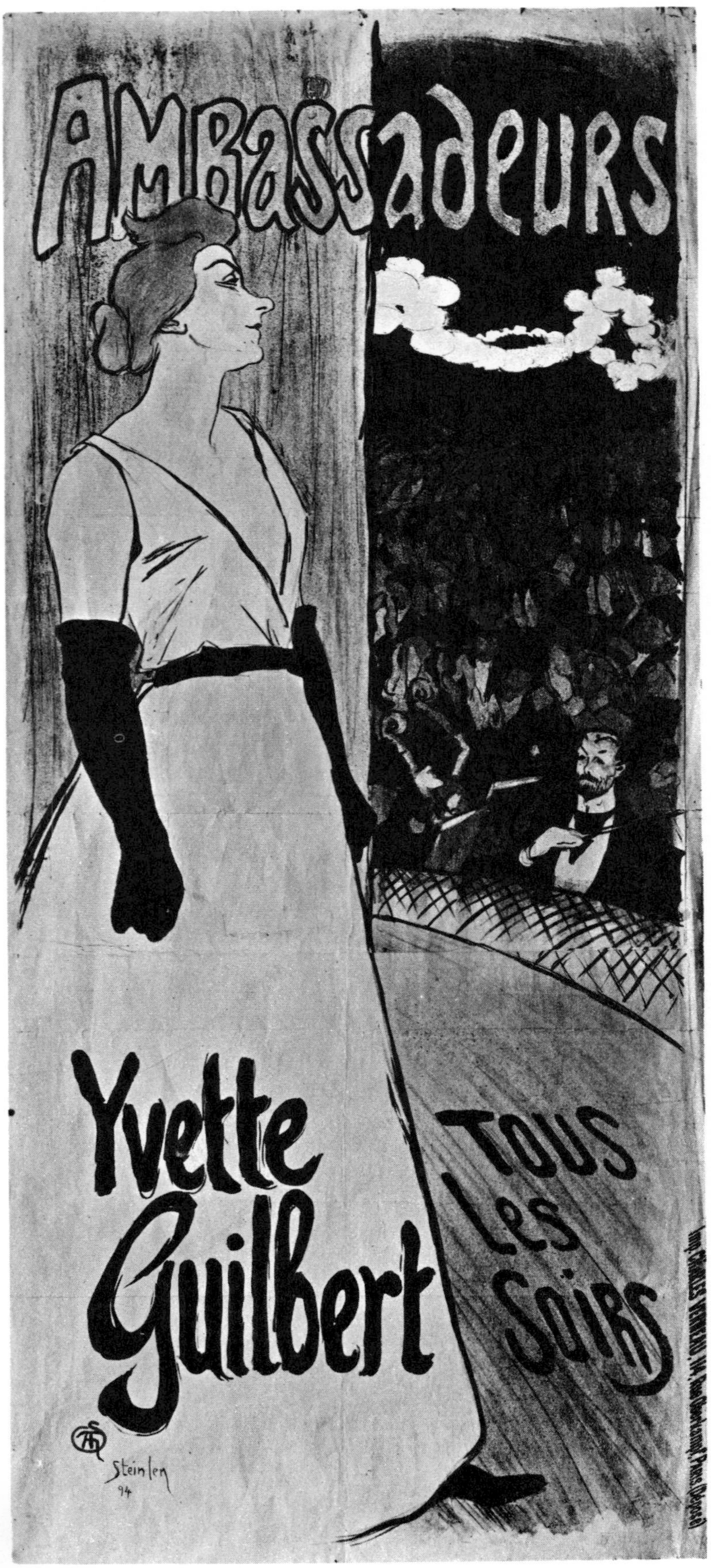

Ambassadeurs
Yvette Guilbert
Tous les Soirs
Steinlen 94
Imp. Charles Verneau, 114, Rue Oberkampf, Paris (Déposé)

5   THEOPHILE-ALEXANDRE STEINLEN (1859-1923)

Le Chat Noir. Lithograph, 55" x 59"

Famous as a meeting place for Verlaine, Zola and Toulouse-Lautrec, *Le Chat Noir* was a cabaret created by Roger de Salis, the self-crowned king of Montmartre. Steinlen, a habitué of the cabaret, designed this cat to embellish any announcement that de Salis wished to make to the Parisian public. The halo around the cat's head is inscribed "Mon Joie, Montmartre".

When the poster first appeared Louis Bazzi wrote "The walls of Paris have been dignified by the presence of this haloed cat, hieratic, Byzantine, of enormous size, whose fantastic silhouette hangs high above the crowd in the streets".

6   ALPHONSE MARIE MUCHA (1860-1939)

Paris 1900. 1899, sketch for poster, indian ink and watercolour (Jiri Mucha)

A Czech by birth, Mucha became established as the leading decorative artist in Paris during the nineties with the posters he designed for Sarah Bernhardt. A fluent and prolific draughtsman, his style epitomized the linear decorative element typical of so much Art Nouveau. This sketch, for the 1900 World Exhibition demonstrates the mastery of line and elegant composition that makes it instantly recognizable as his work, although it lacks many of the essential hallmarks of his style.

7   MAURICE REALIER-DUMAS (1860-1928)

Paris Mode. Colour lithograph, 65⅝" x 22⅝"
(Victoria & Albert Museum)

Realier-Dumas cannot be considered amongst the great French poster artists, but he produced several very competent posters. After studying under Gêrome, he joined the Societé des Artistes Français, receiving several gold medals at the Salon. In 1905, established as a fashionable painter, Realier-Dumas was made chevalier of the Legion d'Honneur.

8   HENRI DE TOULOUSE-LAUTREC (1864-1900)

Reine de Joie. 1892, lithograph, 51" x 35¼"
(Victoria & Albert Museum)

Between them, Chéret and Toulouse-Lautrec created the poster as a
new art form. In contrast to the impressionistic style of his paintings,
Toulouse-Lautrec's posters with their use of flat areas of colour and
emphasis on linear rather than plastic values, both established and
employed the idioms which became typical of Art Nouveau posters.

Reine de Joie
par Victor Joze
chez tous les libraires

Imp. Edw ANCOURT & Cie PARIS

9   HENRI DE TOULOUSE – LAUTREC (1864-1900)

Troupe de Mademoiselle Eglantine. 1896, lithograph, 24¼" x 31½"
(Victoria & Albert Museum)

This poster was designed for Mlle Eglantine's troupe on a visit to
England.

10   EUGENE GRASSET (1841-1917)

Encre Marquet. 1892, lithograph, 29¾" x 21¼"
(Victoria & Albert Museum)

Grasset can be considered the French equivalent of William Morris; in
his work is displayed the conscious historicism, a revival of
mediaevalism to counteract academic classicism, which was one of
the sources of Art Nouveau.

The influence of the Pre-Raphaelites is apparent both in the
composition and treatment of the hair and draperies in this poster.

11   EUGENE GRASSET (1841-1917)

The Grafton Gallery. Lithograph, 23¾" x 17¾"
(Victoria & Albert Museum)

Not primarily a poster artist, one of Grasset's ambitions was to
design stained glass. A stained glass window, now at the *Musée des
Arts Décoratifs* was, in fact, made from this poster which, were it not
for the vastly superior quality of the draughtsmanship, could have
been designed by Morris himself.

12   EUGENE GRASSET (1841-1917)

The Drug Addict. Lithograph, 24" x 16"
(The Piccadilly Gallery, London)

Strikingly different both in execution and conception to the Pre-
Raphaelite calm of most of his posters, Grasset's lithograph of a
tormented heroin addict employs the same convention he established
in his posters, the heavy outline defining mass rather than detail, to
produce an extraordinary tension.

13   WILL BRADLEY (b 1868)

Victor Bicycles. Lithograph, 27" x 40⅞"
(Victoria & Albert Museum)

Will Bradley was one of the greatest American Art Nouveau artists.
Pre-eminent as a poster designer, he also produced and illustrated
books and carried out schemes for interior design. Although Bradley
first made his name in the nineties he managed to outlive the era of
Art Nouveau and was still a highly paid designer in the 1930's.

The division of an area into perspectiveless flat sections by an almost
excessive use of curves shows how much Bradley owes to Beardsley,
but unlike Beardsley whose lines have an organic life of their own,
Bradley's lines merely indicate the boundaries between his
multi-coloured mosaics.

In this poster, Bradley makes no explicit use of the third dimension.
The poster is however in three planes; the girl on the bicycle, the boy
watching her (or, one assumes, watching the bicycle) and the actual
lettering of the poster — for one of Bradley's great qualities as a
poster designer was that his lettering forms an integral part of the
design.

14   WILL BRADLEY (b 1868)

Victor Bicycles. Lithograph

This charming poster for Victor Bicycles, which shows the influence
of Beardsley's curvilinear style was later adapted to advertise
Bar-Lock typewriters.

15   WILL BRADLEY (b 1868)

The Chap-Book, cover. (Victoria & Albert Museum)

Bradley designed five covers for the *Chap-Book*, an art magazine founded in Chicago in 1892.

The *Chap-Book*, as a platform for Art Nouveau, became the American equivalent of *Jugend* or *The Studio*.

16   ALASTAIR (pseudonym for HANS HENNING VOIGHT) (b 1889)

Lulu. Illustration to an edition of *Erdgeist* by Frank Wedekind (Georg Müller Verlag, München)

Alastair, the pseudonym of a German who spent most of his time in England and America, is a curiously enigmatic figure. To some extent he filled a gap left by Beardsley's death. In his introduction to the book containing the illustration overleaf published in 1913, Robert Ross, the doyen of the English decadent, compared him favourably to Picasso.

This illustration of the heroine of Wedekind's two plays, *Erdgeist* and *Die Büchse der Pandora,* graphically expresses the mood of the play in which Lulu, by a complete and total amorality shatters the lives and bourgeois values of a whole succession of men.

17   ALASTAIR (pseudonym for HANS HENNING VOIGHT) (b 1889)

"Ah je t'aime Escamille". Illustration to Carmen, from *Forty-three Drawings by Alastair, with a Note of Exclamation by Robert Ross* published by John Lane in 1914 (The Bodley Head Ltd.).

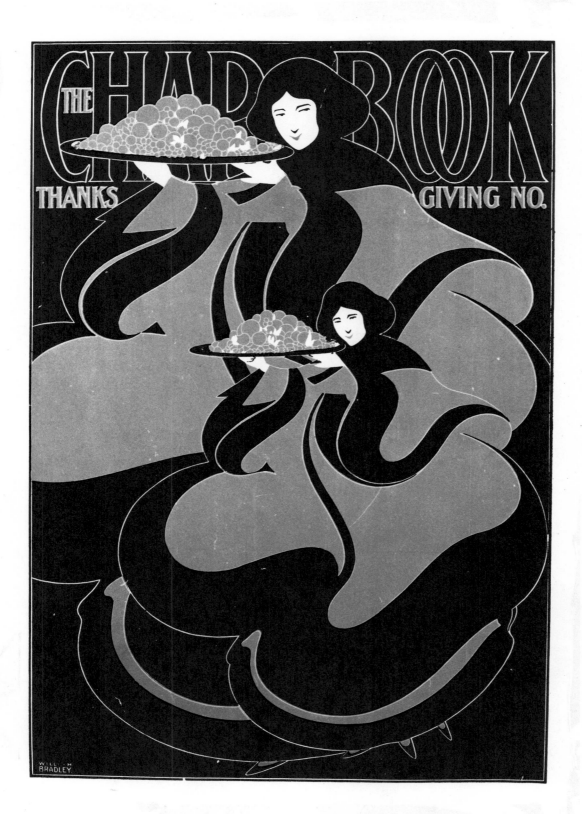

18   RAYMOND PERRY (b 1886)

Cover for The Inland Printer. May 1899, chromo-lithograph,
10¾" x7¾" (Victoria & Albert Museum)

Perry was born near Chicago and studied at the Chicago Institute of
Art. Although he was a noted portrait painter and landscape artist,
he was best known as an illustrator in the style of Bradley.

The Inland Printer, started shortly before the 1893 Exhibition by
McQuilkin, was one of the first magazines to have covers which
changed every week.

19   ROUVILLE

Moulin Rouge. Poster, lithograph from *Les Maîtres de l'Affiche* Paris
1896-1900

20   Book Cover. Anonymous (Victoria & Albert Museum)

This book cover shows how successfully Art Nouveau style could lead itself to a design both abstract and applied.

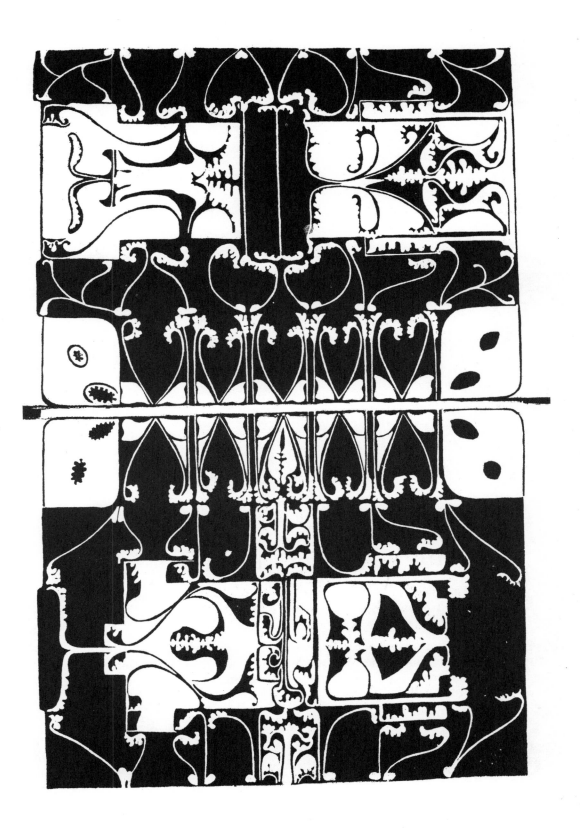

21   WILLIAM THOMAS HORTON (1804-1919)

The Way of a Soul. August 1906, from *William Thomas Horton, a Study of his Work*, Ingpen and Grant 1919.

Horton was an occultist, strongly influenced by Blake. His publication, 'The Way of a Soul' was according to the introduction designed to 'portray the upward struggle of a soul . . . to realisation of the self'.

22   WILLIAM THOMAS HORTON (1864-1919)

The Way of a Soul. June 1910, from *Thomas Horton, a Study of his Work'*, Ingpen and Grant 1919

23   AUBREY VINCENT BEARDSLEY (1872-1898)

Illustration to *'The Houses of Sin'* from *The Later Works of Aubrey Beardsley*, John Lane 1901.

Never has Beardsley's ability to conjure up his convincing fantasy world with a few lines been clearer than in this grotesque imagining.

24   AUBREY VINCENT BEARDSLEY (1872-1898)

The Three Musicians. Vignette to an article in the *Savoy* magazine.

Beardsley was, without doubt, the greatest English exponent of Art Nouveau. He combined all the *fin de siècle* decadence that one associates with Wilde and Whistler and yet is very much part of the nineteenth century artistic tradition in that he was strongly influenced by Burne-Jones and the Pre-Raphaelites and in turn influenced others as diverse as Klimt and Bradley.

The *Savoy* was an art magazine, even more short-lived than the *Yellow Book*

25   AUBREY BEARDSLEY (1872-1898)

Cover for *The Yellow Book*.

In 1894 Beardsley became art editor of *The Yellow Book,* a short-lived periodical devoted to the arts, published by John Lane. It had little to commend it except Beardsley's drawings, and although Wilde had never contributed to the book, its offices (suspected as the headquarters of the 'aesthetic' establishment) were stoned during the first Wilde trial in 1895. Beardsley was then sacked by the management as a scapegoat and as a sop to the indignant public.

26   WILHELM LIST (1864-1918)

Strahlenküsse. 1903, woodcut. (Marlborough Graphics Ltd.)

The Viennese artists who formed the nucleus of Austrian Art Nouveau founded the Wiener Sezession in 1897. This was, more than any other facet of Art Nouveau, a consciously revolutionary movement reacting violently against the traditional academicism of Viennese official art and architecture. The Secession magazine, Ver Sacrum (Sacred Spring) was founded in January 1898 and the first exhibition was held late in the year; it was such a success that Olbrich, one of the foremost Austrian architects, designed the Secession building in Vienna for it. Sezessionstil owed a great deal to English Art Nouveau, the Arts and Crafts movement, and in particular to Charles Rennie Mackintosh of the Glasgow School whose visits to Vienna was prevented by the outbreak of the first world war.

Wilhelm List studied art in Munich and finished his art education in Paris. He was founder member of the Secession. This picture is an illustration to the month June from The Ver Sacrum special calendar issue for 1903.

27   FRANZ WACIK (1883-1939)

The Midnight Feast. Lithograph, 19½" x 15½"
(Marlborough Graphics Ltd)

Wacik, who lived all his life in Vienna was especially noted as a decorator; he frescoed the walls of the Secession building, although as this illustration shows he had a phantasmagoric style all his own.

The Yellow Book

An Illustrated Quarterly

Volume II July 1894

London: Elkin Mathews & John Lane
Boston: Copeland & Day

Price
5/-
Net

28   CARL MOLL (1861-1945)

Hohe Wart. Woodcut, 9⅞" x 9½" (Marlborough Graphics Ltd.)

Moll was a founder member of the Secession and a close friend of Klimt. He was a pupil of the Viennese Academy and his early paintings show the influence of his teacher there, the naturalist painter, Schindler. His later paintings tend to be more impressionist in style.

This woodcut is of a suburb in his native Vienna.

29   LEOPOLD STOLBA (1863-1929)

Girl under a Tree. 1906, woodcut, 11¾" x 8¾"
(Marlborough Graphics Ltd.)

Stolba was a noted portrait painter and sculptor, but is best known
now for his caricatures.

30   FRIEDRICH KONIG (18561941)

Jupiter. Woodcut, 10⅛" x 9½" (Marlborough Graphics Ltd.)

This illustration forms the cover of the *Ver Sacrum* calendar for 1903.

SONDERHEFT

VER SACRUM
KALENDER
1903

PREIS 2 K

31   FERDINAND ANDRI (1871-1956)

December. Woodcut from 'Ver Sacrum' calendar
(Marlborough Graphics Ltd.)

Andri was born in Vienna and studied at the Academy there. He
finished his art education at Carlsruhe. On his return to Vienna,
Andri became known as a lithographer and sculptor but especially as
a painter of peasant life.

32   RUDOLF JETTMAR (1869-1939)

Roman Ruins in Schönbrunn. Engraving, 8½" x 7"
(Marlborough Graphics Ltd.)

Jettmar was born in Poland but worked in Vienna. He exhibited at
the Paris Exhibition of 1900.

33   ANGELO JANK (1868-1940)

Cover for *Jugend*. Colour Process Engraving, 10¾" x 8¼"
(Victoria & Albert Museum)

One of the most active centres of Art Nouveau in Europe was
Munich. In 1892 the Munich Secession was founded by Franz von
Stuck and others, and in 1896 Georg Horth (a member of the Vienna
Secession) started the magazine *Jugend* which soon gave its name to
the German Art Nouveau movement — Jugendstil.

Jank was a prominent member of the Secession. In 1899 he formed
the group Die Scholle. He exhibited considerably before the first
world war and drew several covers for *Jugend*.

34　　OTTO ECKMANN (1865-1902)

Cover for *Jugend*. Colour process engraving, 9¼" x 7⅜"
(Victoria & Albert Museum)

Eckmann was the foremost member of the German Art Nouveau
movement. He was born in Hamburg where he was strongly
influenced by Justus Brinkmann, founder of the Museum fur Kunst
und Gewerbe, but studied and spent most of his life in Munich.
Apart from covers for Jugend such as this, Eckmann designed
wallpapers and tapestries, illustrated books and created the most
important Art Nouveau type face — Eckmann type. His own art
collection, mostly of works by his Art Nouveau contemporaries was
left to Brinkmann's museum in Hamburg.

35   LEOPOLD STOLBA (1863-1929)

February. Woodcut from 'Ver Sacrum' calendar
(Marlborough Graphics Ltd.)

36   OTTO ECKMANN (1865-1902)

The Crab. Jugend 1899 (The Piccadilly Gallery, London)

37   OWEN JONES (1809-1874)

Wallpaper. 1852 (Victoria & Albert Museum)

Owen Jones, responsible for the decoration of the Great Exhibition
of 1881, was one of the best interior designers of his day. He studied
at the Royal Academy, travelled to the East where he took a great
interest in oriental art. His flat geometric style and his rejection of
the vulgar, blowsy, cabbage-like forms of early Victorian wallpapers
did a great deal to pave the way for Art Nouveau, of which he may
be considered a precursor. He wrote in 'The Grammar of Ornament'
(1856) "The world has become weary of the eternal repetition of the
same conventional forms that have passed away".

38   Roller-printed cotton cloth by F. Steiner and Co. 1903
(Victoria & Albert Museum)

39   Roller-printed figured cloth by Turnbull and Stockdale Ltd c.1900
(Victoria & Albert Museum)

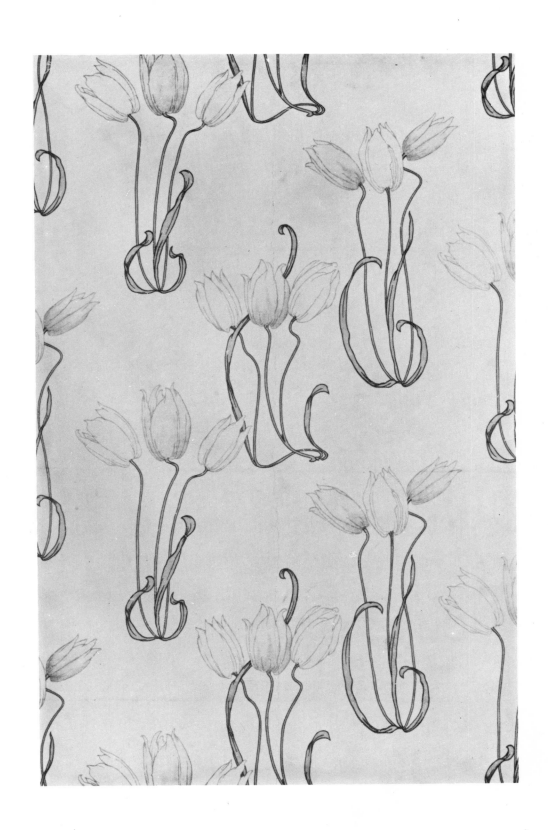

40 CHARLES ANNESLEY VOYSEY (1857-1941)

Decorative Fabric. 1897, manufactured by Newman, Smith and Newman (Victoria & Albert Museum)

Best known as an architect, Voysey's small country houses made him one of the most sought-after architects of the 1890's. The simple lines and informal designs (from the inside working outwards) were revolutionary compared to the fussy ornamentation of Victorian architecture. Voysey however was as active a designer of textiles as he was an architect. He first started designing fabrics in 1884. By 1890 he was one of the most successful designers in the country.

41   ARTHUR HEYGATE MACKMURDO

Decorative Fabric. 1883 (Victoria & Albert Museum)

This fabric was designed in the same year as 'Wren's City Churches'
and is just as much ahead of its time.

42   ARTHUR HEYGATE MACKMURDO (1854-1942)

Wren's City Churches. 1883, woodcut. (Victoria & Albert Museum)

Mackmurdo probably more than any other person gave the impetus to the new movement that was to be Art Nouveau. The book cover shown here is probably the first manifestation of Art Nouveau as it has come to be understood in the decorative, floral, Western European style. All the elements which were to be so popular ten years later are here — stylised flowers with long, slender stalks, type design that is part of the ornament and a complete absence of perspective.

WRENS CITY & CHURCHES

BY
A·H·MACKMURDO, A·R·I·B·A,
1883
G.ALLEN, SUNNYSIDE, ORPINGTON, KENT.

43 ARTHUR HEYGATE MACKMURDO (1854-1942)

The Century Guild Hobby Horse (The Studio)

The Century Guild Hobby Horse was the magazine of the Century Guild, a group of artist-craftmen, started by Mackmurdo with Selwyn Image and William de Morgan in order to propagate their new decorative style.

44   CHARLES RICKETTS (1866-1931)

The Nimphidia and the Muses Elizium. The Studio, October 1896,
title page for a book published by the Vale Press, 1896 by
M. Drayton

Ricketts who was strongly influenced by the aesthetic movement was
gifted as a painter, sculptor and writer. He was a great admirer of
Morris and the Japanese graphic tradition. In 1896 he founded the
Vale Press where he designed founts, initials and borders, many of
which, like this one showing the influence of Dürer's woodcuts.

45, 46 ORNAMENTAL LETTERS from 'The Studio' 'Art Nouveau',
Dover Publications Ltd. New York

'The Studio', a monthly magazine published in London from 1893
was one of the most influential propagators of Art Nouveau. It did a
great deal to encourage the new graphic style by holding
competitions for the design of relatively simple subjects. These two
plates show the results of competition that were published in
August 1894 and October 1894.

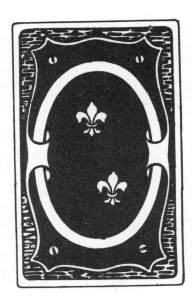

47   JESSIE M. KING (1872-1948)

The Dryad of the Trees (The Fine Art Society Ltd)

Jessie M. King was a member of the Glasgow School
with Mackmurdo. She was also a very accomplished illustrator of
children's books.

THE DRYAD OF THE TREES

48   JESSIE M. KING (1872-1948)

'Her Face was veiled with a Veil of Gauze . . .' 1905, ink and wash 10¾" x 8¾" (Miss Anne Barren).

HER·FACE·WAS·VEILED·WITH·A·VEIL·OF·GAUZE·BUT·HER·FEET·WERE·NAKED·

49   CHARLES ROBINSON (b 1871)

Thinking of Little Alice. 1904, from *Alice's Adventures in Wonderland* (Cassell and Co. Ltd)

Charles Robinson was one of the foremost book illustrators of his day. What is interesting about this illustration is the extraordinary convolution of the flowers in the foreground which are superb examples of the narcissistic style of late Art Nouveau — hardly ever equalled except in textile designs. (See plates 38 and 39)

Thinking of little Alice

50 WALTER CRANE (1845-1901)

The Daffodil. Illustration to *Flora's Feast*

Crane, like Mackmurdo was a fore-runner of Art Nouveau. Despite his importance in the development of the movement, he was never closely associated with other Art Nouveau artists. Most of his work consists of illustrations for children's books — he produced many with Kate Greenaway — although he worked with Burne-Jones, Morris and Ashbee in the hope of reforming decorative and applied art.

The Daffodil his trumpet blows,
And after Spring a
hunting
goes.

51   WALTER CRANE (1845-1901)

The Lilies. Illustration to *Flora's Feast*.

Then lilies, turned to Tigers, blaze
Amid the garden's tangled maze.

52   CHARLES RICKETTS (1866–1931)

The Moon-Horned Io. Woodcut, Illustration to
'The Sphinx' by Oscar Wilde, London 1894.

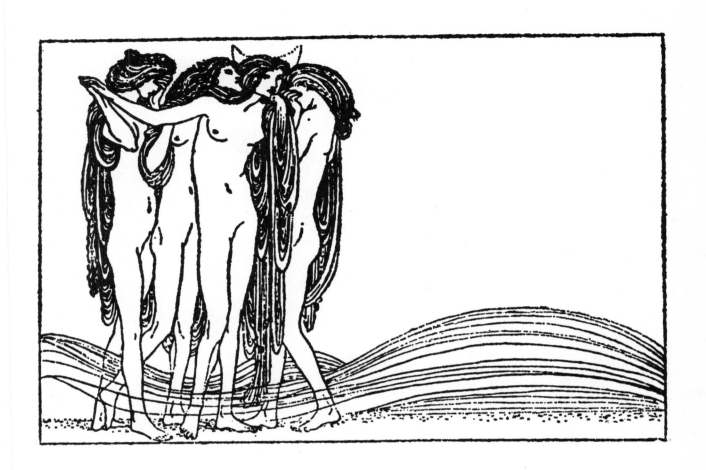

FARNHAM SCHOOL OF ART